Name: _____

Say It Loud!

Affirmation ABC's And

HANDWRITING PRACTICE

I AM...

Aa Aa Aa Aa Aa Aa

Able Able Able Able

Definition: Having the power or skill that is needed to do something

Kyla Thompson

Enhanced DNA

DEVELOP. NURTURE. ACHIEVE.
Publishing Division

www.EnhancedDNAPublishing.com
DenolaBurton@EnhancedDNA1.com
317-537-1438

Say It Loud!: Affirmation ABC's and Handwriting Practice

Cover Design: Md. Rahibul Islam

ISBN-13: 978-1-7369079-7-9

ABOUT THE AUTHOR

Kyla Thompson is passionate about helping others to become more confident through the power of their words. As a mother of two daughters, she understands the value of instilling mindfulness practices, such as affirmations, early in life. She strives to create impact through her volunteer efforts with organizations such as Girls Inc., Girls Who Brunch Tour, and Pink-4-Ever Inc. She has authored and co-authored two books, two short-stories, and an e-book. She is currently studying to obtain a master's degree in Clinical Mental Health Counseling. Download a FREE affirmation printable and learn more information about special pricing for bulk orders at www.AffirmationABC.com.

A a

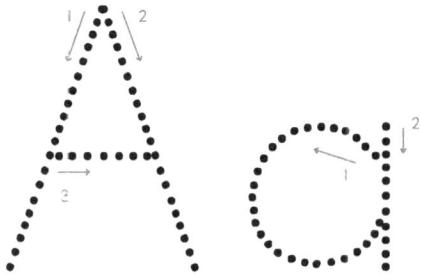

is for afro-puffs.

Trace the letters with a pencil.

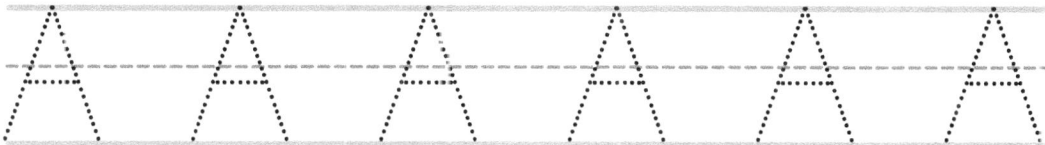

A A A A A A

Trace the letters with a pencil.

a a a a a a

Trace the letters with a pencil.

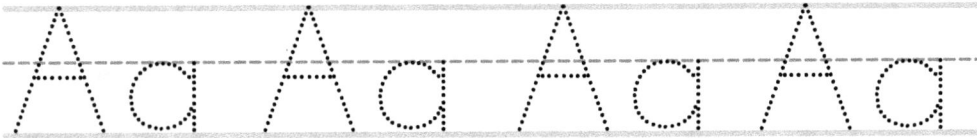

Aa Aa Aa Aa

A

a

A

a

Instructions: Have your child trace the word, say the word out loud, and help to read the definition of each word. You can even hang this on their wall or mirror to say each day as a daily affirmation.

A

I am...

Trace the letters with a pencil.

Able

Definition: Having the power or skill that is needed to do something.

Amazing

Definition: Causing great surprise or wonder.

Awesome

Definition: Extremely good.

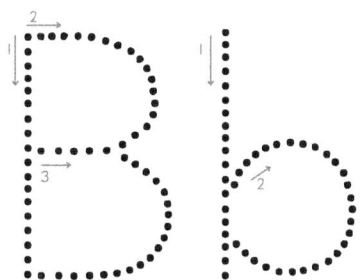

B b

is for boy.

Trace the letters with a pencil.

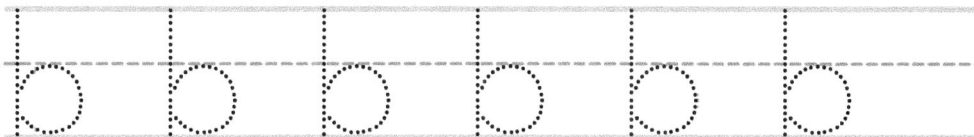

B B B B B B

Trace the letters with a pencil.

b b b b b b

Trace the letters with a pencil.

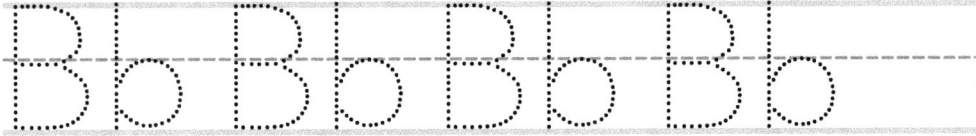

Bb Bb Bb Bb Bb

B

b

B

b

Instructions: Have your child trace the word, say the word out loud, and help to read the definition of each word. You can even hang this on the r wall or mirror to say each day as a daily affirmation.

B

I am...

Beautiful

Definition: Having beauty, very good or pleasing.

Bold

Definition: Not afraid of cifficult situations; showing confidence.

Brilliant

Definition: Very impressive or successful; extremely intelligent.

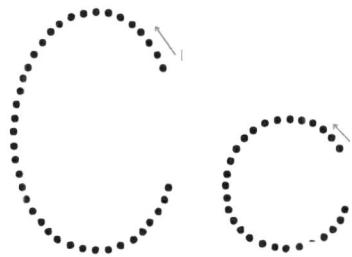

C c

is for crown.

Trace the letters with a pencil.

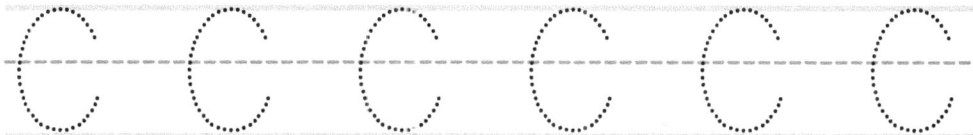

C C C C C C

Trace the letters with a pencil.

c c c c c c c

Trace the letters with a pencil.

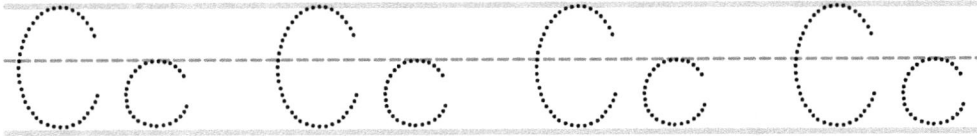

Cc   Cc   Cc   Cc

C

c

C

C

Instructions: Have your child trace the word, say the word out loud, and help to read the definition of each word. You can even hang this on their wall or mirror to say each day as a daily affirmation.

C

I am...

Caring

Definition: Feeling or showing concern for other people.

Creative

Definition: Using the ability to make or think of new things.

Courageous

Definition: Very brave.

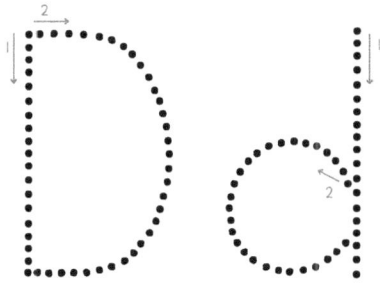

D d

is for doctor.

Trace the letters with a pencil.

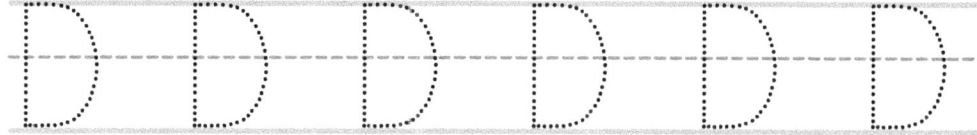

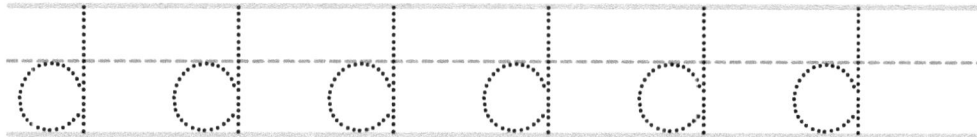

D   D   D   D   D   D

Trace the letters with a pencil.

d   d   d   d   d   d

Trace the letters with a pencil.

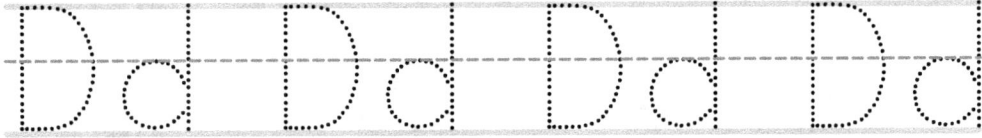

Dd Dd Dd Dd

D

d

D

d

Instructions: Have your child trace the word, say the word out loud, and help to read the definition of each word. You can even hang this on their wall or mirror to say each day as a daily affirmation.

D

I am...

Daring

Definition: Showing lack of fear.

Deserving

Definition: Should have or be given something.

Determined

Definition: Having a strong feeling that you are going to do something and that you will not allow anyone or anything to stop you.

E e

is for earth.

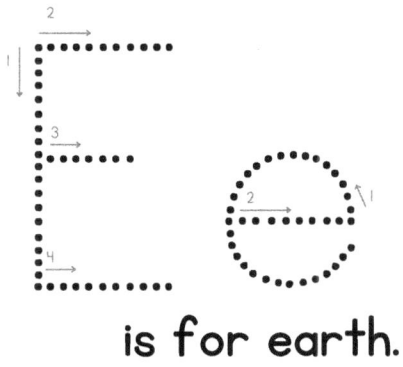

Trace the letters with a pencil.

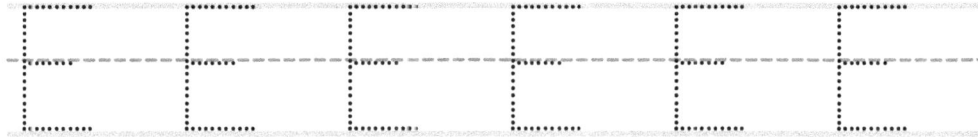

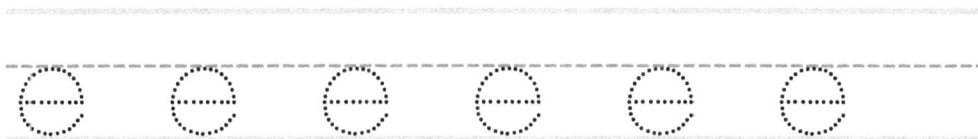

E E E E E

Trace the letters with a pencil.

e e e e e e

Trace the letters with a pencil.

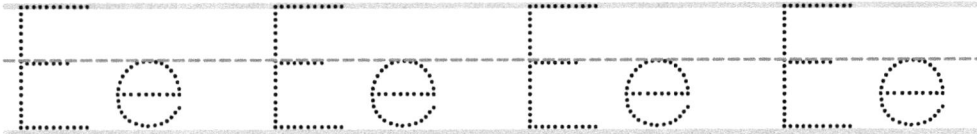

Ee Ee Ee Ee

E

e

E

e

Instructions: Have your child trace the word, say the word out loud, and help to read the definition of each word. You can even hang this on their wall or mirror to say each day as a daily affirmation.

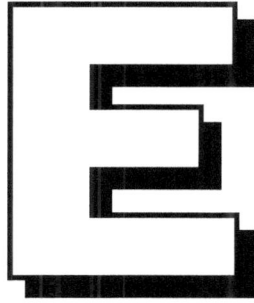

E

I am...

Energetic

Definition: Having or showing a lot energy.

Encouraged

Definition: To make more hopeful or confident.

Excellent

Definition: Very good.

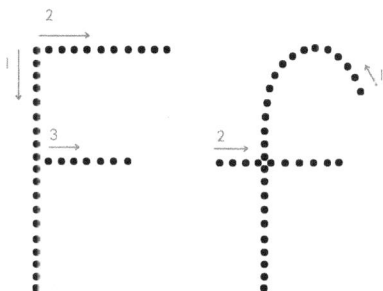

is for fish.

Trace the letters with a pencil.

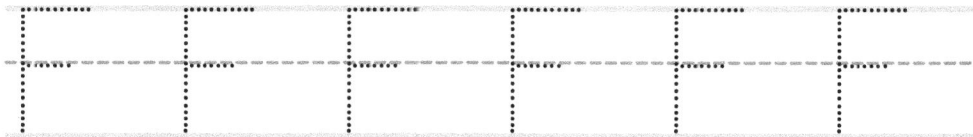

Trace the letters with a pencil.

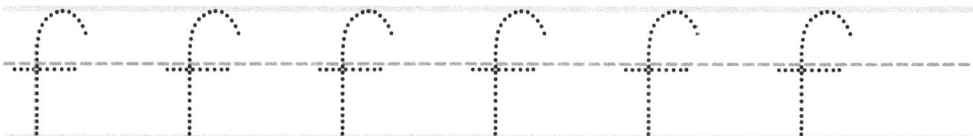

Trace the letters with a pencil.

F f   F f   F f   F f   F f   F f

F

f

F

f

Instructions: Have your child trace the word, say the word out loud, and help to read the definition of each word. You can even hang this on their wall or mirror to say each day as a daily affirmation.

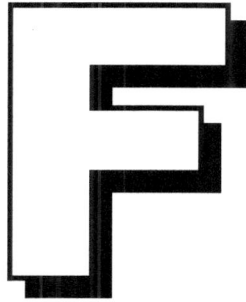

F

I am...

Fun

Definition: Someone or something that is amusing or enjoyable.

Fearless

Definition: Not afraid; very brave..

Friendly

Definition: Showing support; kind and helpful.

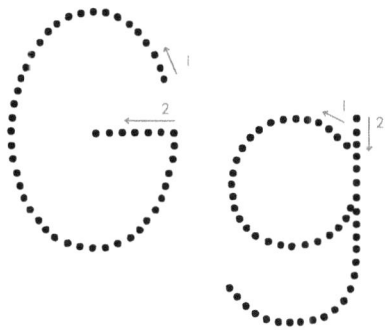

Gg

is for grapes.

Trace the letters with a pencil.

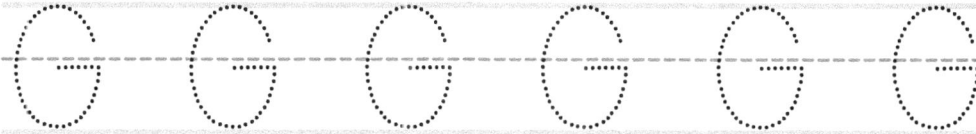

G G G G G G

Trace the letters with a pencil.

g g g g g g

Trace the letters with a pencil.

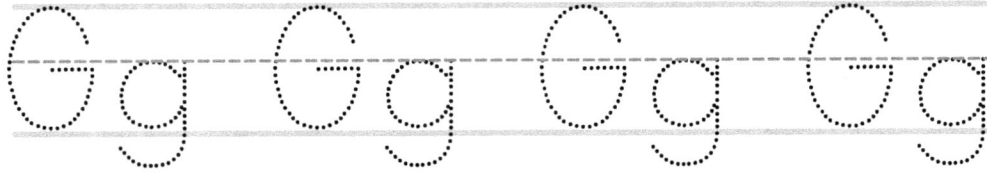

Gg Gg Gg Gg Gg

G

g

G

g

Instructions: Have your child trace the word, say the word out loud, and help to read the definition of each word. You can even hang this on their wall or mirror to say each day as a daily affirmation.

G

I am...

Great

Definition: Better than good; very important, talented or successful.

Gifted

Definition: Having great natural ability.

Grateful

Definition: Feeling or showing thanks.

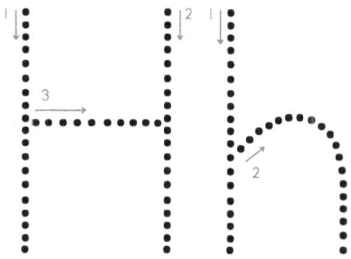

Hh

is for hand.

Trace the letters with a pencil.

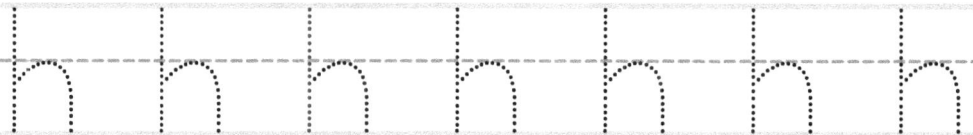

Trace the letters with a pencil.

Kyla Thompson

Trace the letters with a pencil.

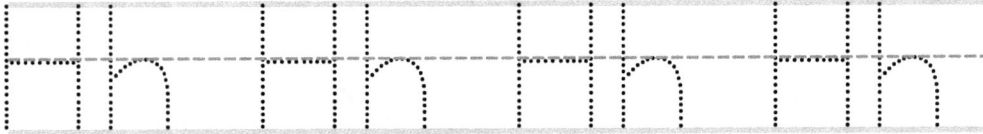

30

Instructions: Have your child trace the word, say the word out loud, and help to read the definition of each word. You can even hang this on their wall or mirror to say each day as a daily affirmation.

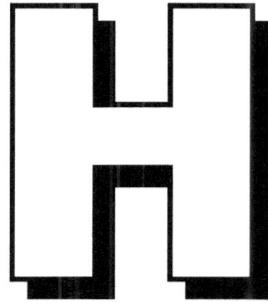

H

I am...

Happy

Definition: Feelng pleasure and enjoyment because of your life, situation, etc..

Healthy

Definition: Having good health, not sick or injured; doing well.

Hopeful

Definition: Full of hope; wanting something to happen or be true..

I i

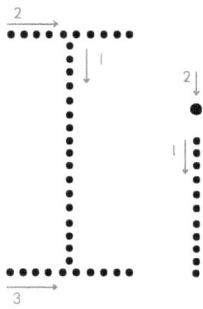

is for ice cream.

Trace the letters with a pencil.

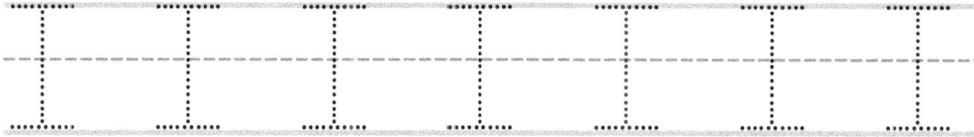

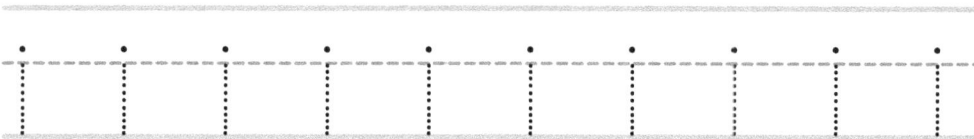

Trace the letters with a pencil.

Trace the letters with a pencil.

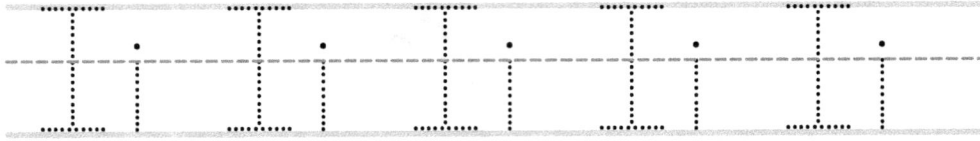

Ii Ii Ii Ii Ii Ii

I

i

I

i

Instructions: Have your child trace the word, say the word out loud, and help to read the definition of each word. You can even hang this on their wall or mirror to say each day as a daily affirmation.

I am...

Intelligent

Definition: Able to learn and understand things.

Incredible

Definition: Extremely good, great or large.

Important

Definition: Having serious meaning or worth; having power or influence.

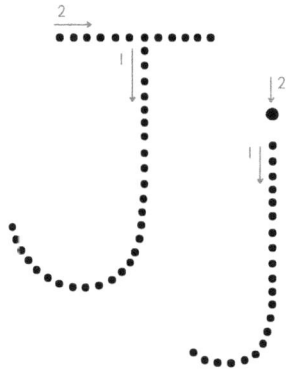

J j

is for jacket.

Trace the letters with a pencil.

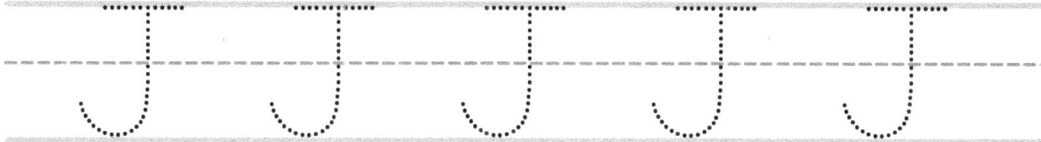

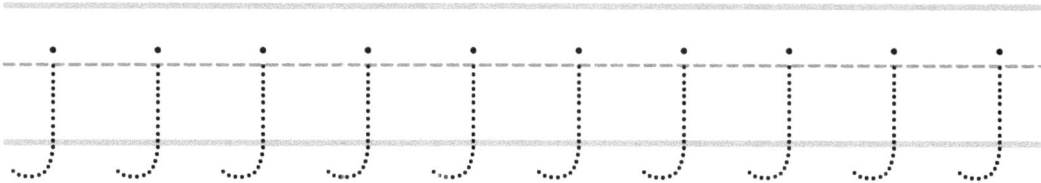

J J J J J

Trace the letters with a pencil.

j j j j j j j j j j

Trace the letters with a pencil.

Jj Jj Jj Jj

J

j

J

j

Instructions: Have your child trace the word, say the word out loud, and help to read the definition of each word. You can even hang this on their wall or mirror to say each day as a daily affirmation.

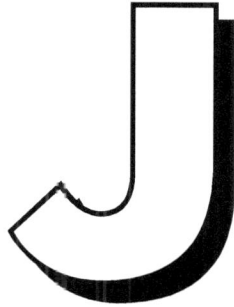

J

I am...

Jolly

Definition: Full of happiness and cheerful.

Joyful

Definition: Feeling, causing or showing great happiness.

Jazzy

Definition: Bright, lively or fancy in a way that is meant to attract attention.

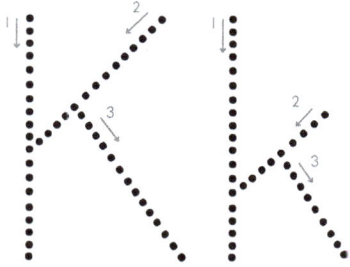

K k

is for king.

Trace the letters with a pencil.

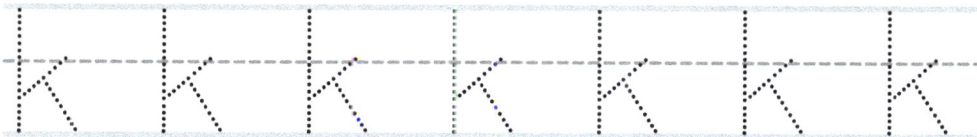

K K K K K K K

Trace the letters with a pencil.

k k k k k k k

Trace the letters with a pencil.

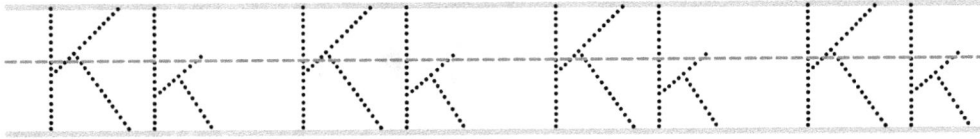

Kk Kk Kk Kk

K

k

K

k

Instructions: Have your child trace the word, say the word out loud, and help to read the definition of each word. You can even hang this on their wall or mirror to say each day as a daily affirmation.

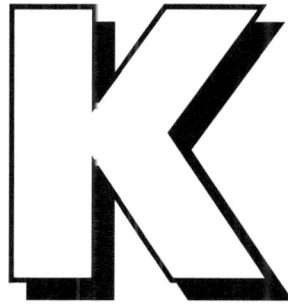

K

I am...

Kind

Definition: Wanting and liking to do good things to bring happiness to others.

Kingly

Definition: Of or relating to a king.

Knowledgable

Definition: Having information or understanding.

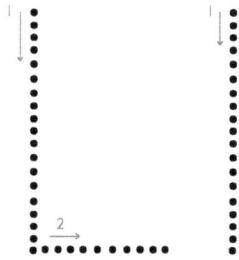

is for lion.

Trace the letters with a pencil.

Trace the letters with a pencil.

Trace the letters with a pencil.

Instructions: Have your child trace the word, say the word out loud, and help to read the definition of each word. You can even hang this on their wall or mirror to say each day as a daily affirmation.

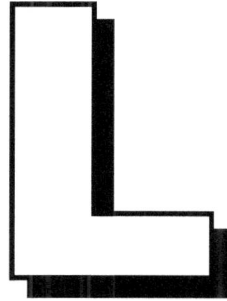

L

I am...

Loved

Definition: A feeling of strong or constant caring for someone.

Learning

Definition: The process of gaining knowledge or skill by studying, practice or being taught.

Loyal

Definition: Having or showing complete and constant support for someone or something..

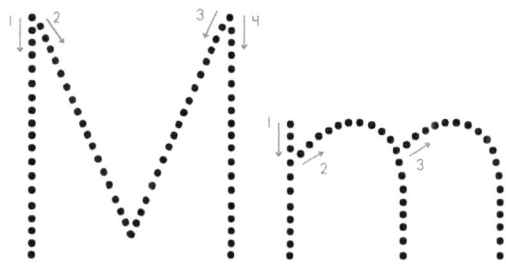

Mm

is for milk.

Trace the letters with a pencil.

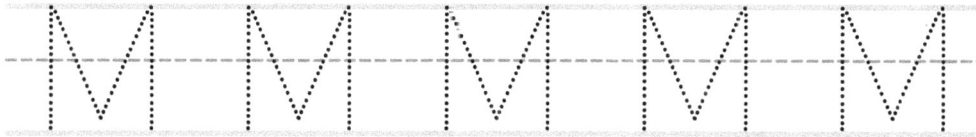

M M M M M M

Trace the letters with a pencil.

m m m m m

Trace the letters with a pencil.

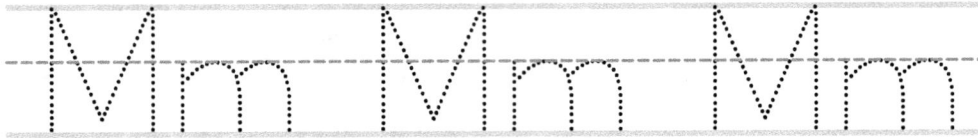

Mm Mm Mm

M

m

M

m

Instructions: Have your child trace the word, say the word out loud, and help to read the definition of each word. You can even hang this on their wall or mirror to say each day as a daily affirmation.

M

I am...

Mighty

Definition: Having or showing great strength.

Mindful

Definition: Aware of something that may be important.

Motivating

Definition: To give someone or be a reason for doing something.

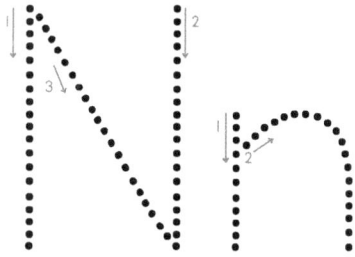

Nn

is for nurse.

Trace the letters with a pencil.

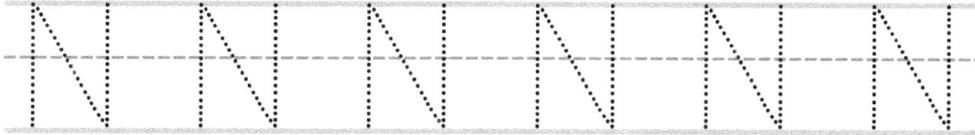

N N N N N N

Trace the letters with a pencil.

n n n n n n

Trace the letters with a pencil.

Nn Nn Nn Nn

N

n

N

n

Instructions: Have your child trace the word, say the word out loud, and help to read the definition of each word. You can even hang this on their wall or mirror to say each day as a daily affirmation.

N

I am...

Nice

Definition: Kind, polite and friendly.

Neat

Definition: Clean and orderly.

Nimble

Definition: Able to move quickly, easily and lightly.

O o

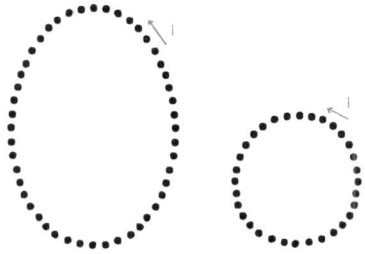

is for octopus.

Trace the letters with a pencil.

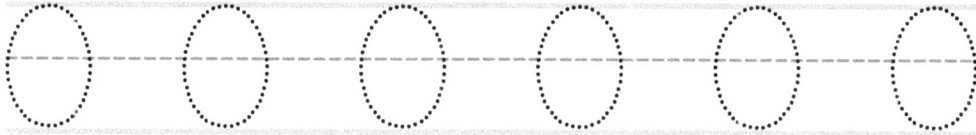

Trace the letters with a pencil.

Trace the letters with a pencil.

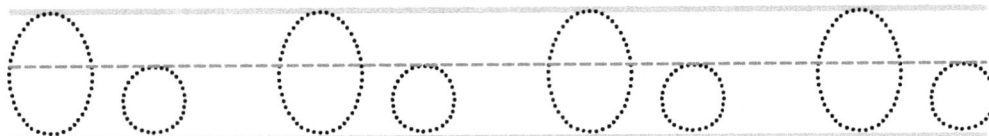

Oo Oo Oo Oo

O

o

O

o

Instructions: Have your child trace the word, say the word out loud, and help to read the definition of each word. You can even hang this on their wall or mirror to say each day as a daily affirmation.

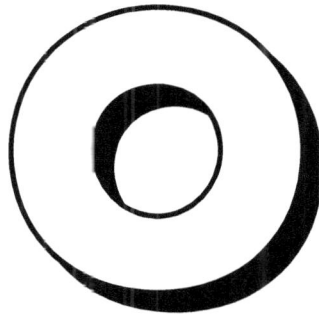

O

I am...

Overjoyed

Definition: Very happy.

Optimistic

Definition: Having or showing hope for the future; expecting good things to happen.

Outstanding

Definition: Extremely good or excellent.

is for pineapple.

Trace the letters with a pencil.

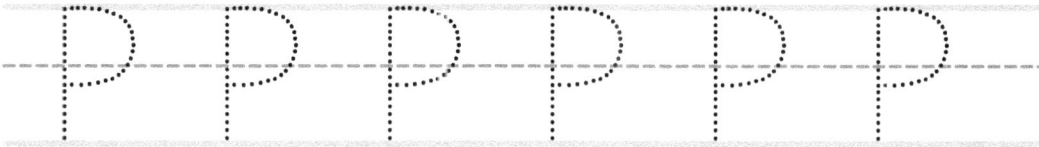

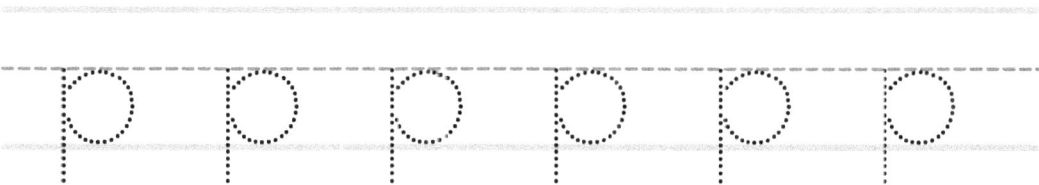

Trace the letters with a pencil.

Trace the letters with a pencil.

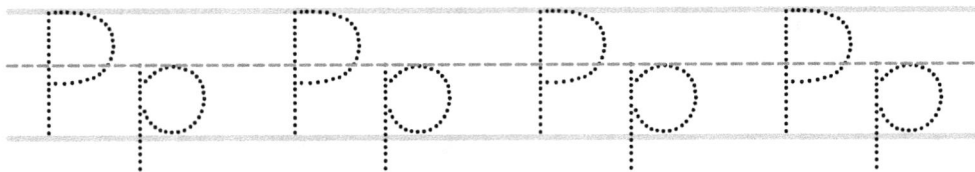

P p P p P p P p

P

p

P

p

Instructions: Have your child trace the word, say the word out loud, and help to read the definition of each word. You can even hang this on their wall or mirror to say each day as a daily affirmation.

P

I am...

Proud

Definition: Very happy and pleased because of something you have done, something you own, someone you know or are related to.

Peaceful

Definition: Quiet and calm.

Patient

Definition: Able to remain calm when waiting for a long time or when dealing with problems or difficult people.

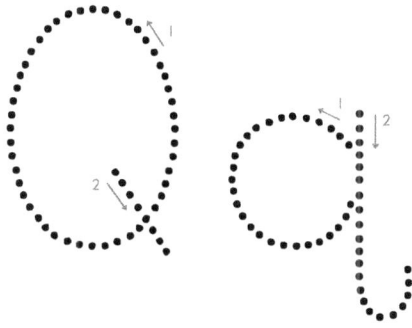

Q q

is for queen.

Trace the letters with a pencil.

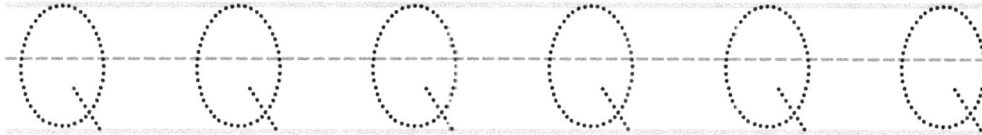

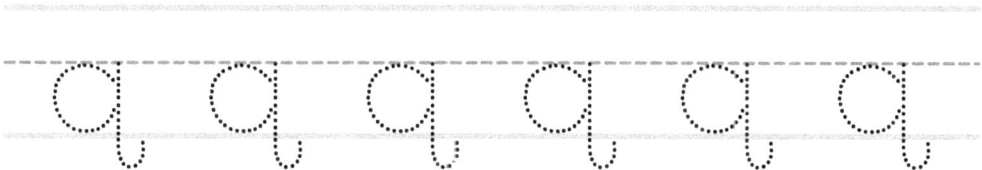

Q Q Q Q Q Q

Trace the letters with a pencil.

q q q q q q

Trace the letters with a pencil.

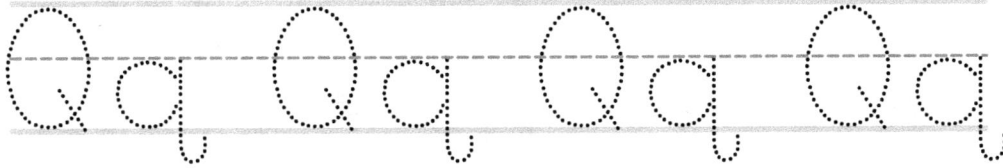

Qq Qq Qq Qq

Q

q

Q

q

Instructions: Have your child trace the word, say the word out loud, and help to read the definition of each word. You can even hang this on their wall or mirror to say each day as a daily affirmation.

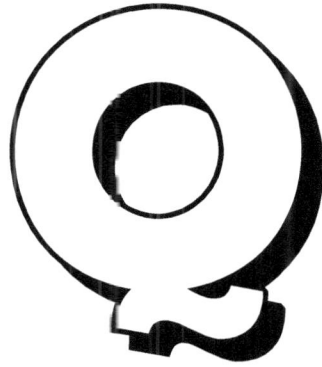

Q

I am...

Quick

Definition: Fast in thinking, learning or understanding.

Queenly

Definition: Resembling a queen or suitable for a queen.

Quirky

Definition: Different in an interesting or appealing way.

Rr

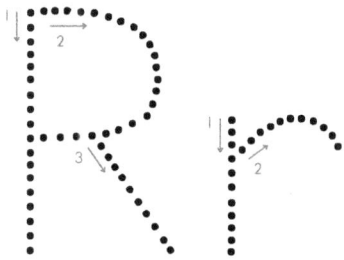

is for rainbow.

Trace the letters with a pencil.

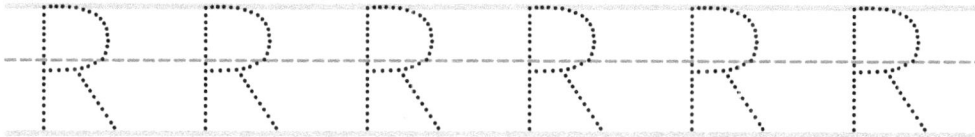

R R R R R R

Trace the letters with a pencil.

r r r r r r r

Trace the letters with a pencil.

R r R r R r R r

R

r

R

r

Instructions: Have your child trace the word, say the word out loud, and help to read the definition of each word. You can even hang this on their wall or mirror to say each day as a daily affirmation.

R

I am...

Respectful

Definition: Showing someone or something is good, valuable, or important.

Reliable

Definition: Able to be trusted to do or provide what is needed.

Relaxed

Definition: Comfortable, calm and free from stress, worry, or anxiety.

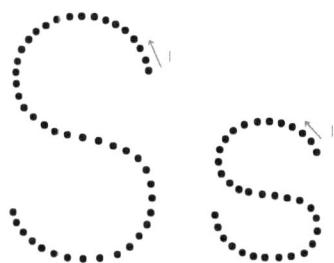

Ss

is for sun.

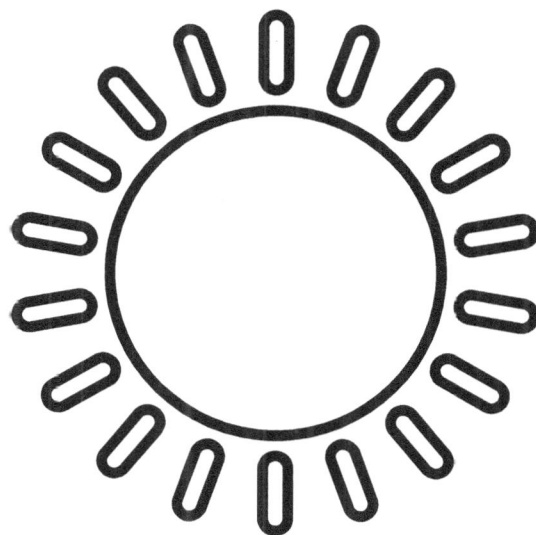

Trace the letters with a pencil.

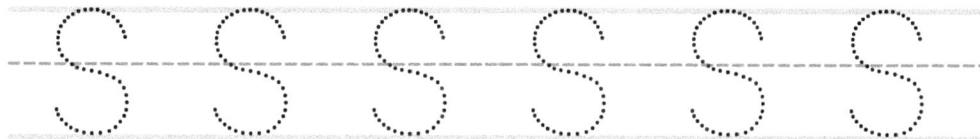

S S S S S S

Trace the letters with a pencil.

S S S S S S S

Trace the letters with a pencil.

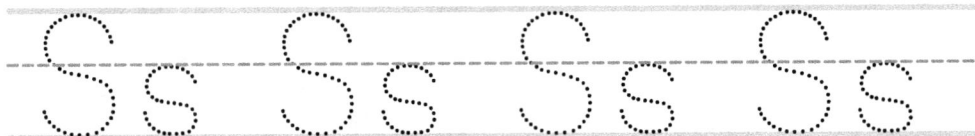

Ss Ss Ss Ss

S

s

S

s

Instructions: Have your child trace the word, say the word out loud, and help to read the definition of each word. You can even hang this on their wall or mirror to say each day as a daily affirmation.

S

I am...

Safe

Definition: Protected from hurt, harm, and danger.

Strong

Definition: Having great physical power and ability, very confident and able to deal with difficult situations.

Successful

Definition: Having the correct or desired result, having gotten or achieved wealth, respect or fame.

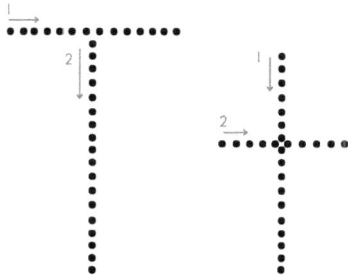

is for tree.

Trace the letters with a pencil.

Trace the letters with a pencil.

Trace the letters with a pencil.

Instructions: Have your child trace the word, say the word out loud, and help to read the definition of each word. You can even hang this on their wall or mirror to say each day as a daily affirmation.

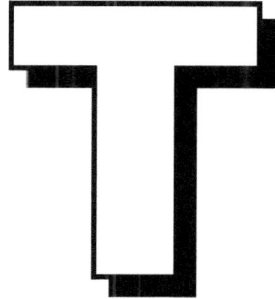

T

I am...

Talented

Definition: Having a special ability to do something well.

Transforming

Definition: Changing completely and usually in a good way.

Truthful

Definition: Telling the real facts about something, honest.

Uu

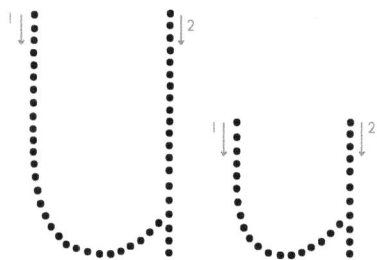

is for umbrella.

Trace the letters with a pencil.

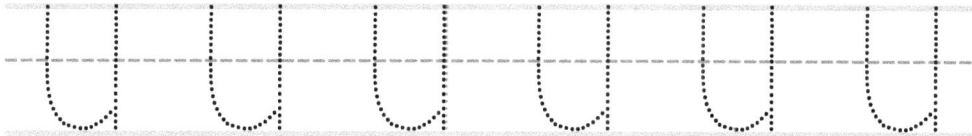

U U U U U U

Trace the letters with a pencil.

u u u u u u u

Trace the letters with a pencil.

Uu Uu Uu Uu

U

U

U

U

Instructions: Have your child trace the word, say the word out loud, and help to read the definition of each word. You can even hang this on their wall or mirror to say each day as a daily affirmation.

U

I am...

Unique

Definition: Unlike anything or anyone else, one of a kind.

Upright

Definition: Always behaving in an honest way.

Unstoppable

Definition: Not able to be stopped.

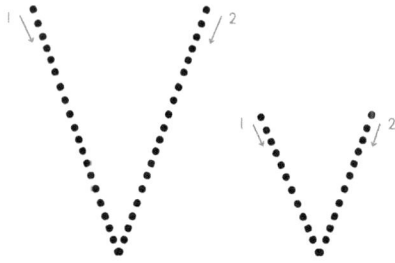

V v

is for violin.

Trace the letters with a pencil.

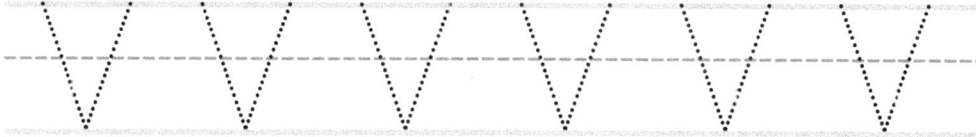

V V V V V V

Trace the letters with a pencil.

V V V V V V V

Trace the letters with a pencil.

V V V V V V V V V V V V

V

V

V

V

Instructions: Have your child trace the word, say the word out loud, and help to read the definition of each word. You can even hang this on their wall or mirror to say each day as a daily affirmation.

V

I am...

Vibrant

Definition: Having or showing great energy; very bright and strong.

Victorious

Definition: Having success in defeating an opponent or enemy.

Valued

Definition: useful or important.

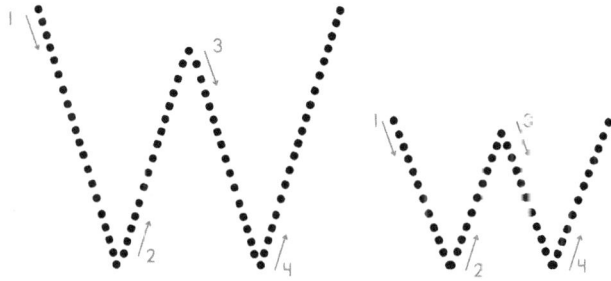

W w

is for whale.

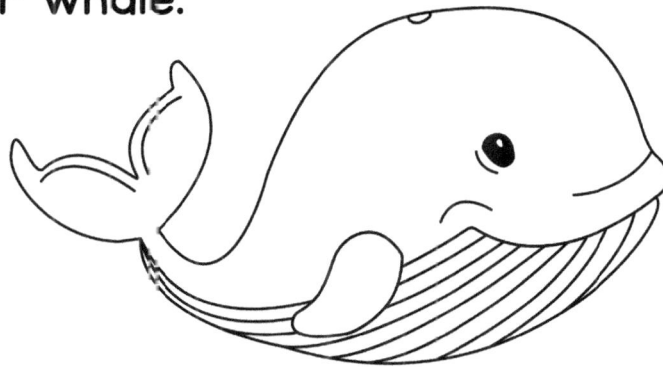

Trace the letters with a pencil.

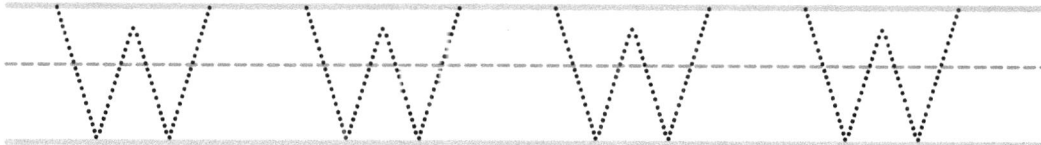

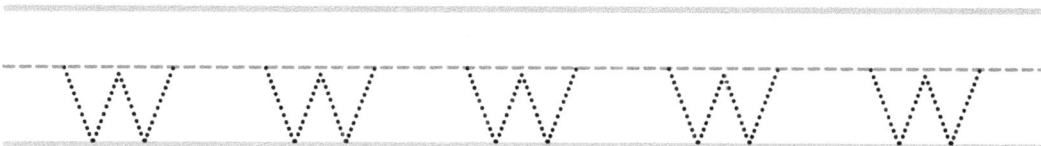

Trace the letters with a pencil.

Trace the letters with a pencil.

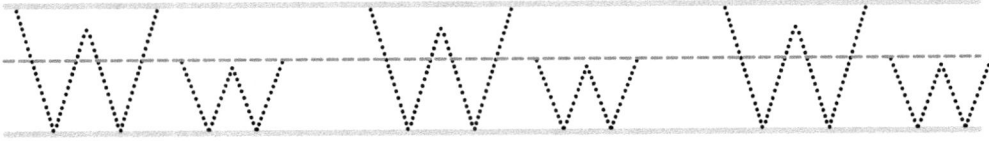

W W w W W w W W w

W

W

W

W

Instructions: Have your child trace the word, say the word out loud, and help to read the definition of each word. You can even hang this on their wall or mirror to say each day as a daily affirmation.

W

I am...

Worthy

Definition: Good and deserving respect, praise or attention.

Well-behaved

Definition: Acting in a polite or correct manner.

Wonderful

Definition: Extremely good.

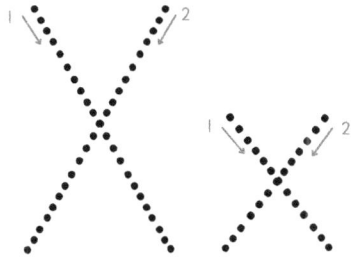

X x

is for x-ray.

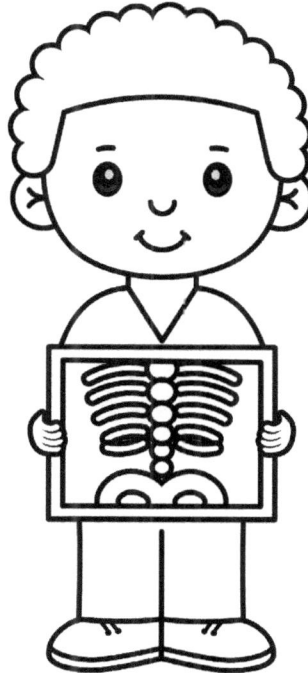

Trace the letters with a pencil.

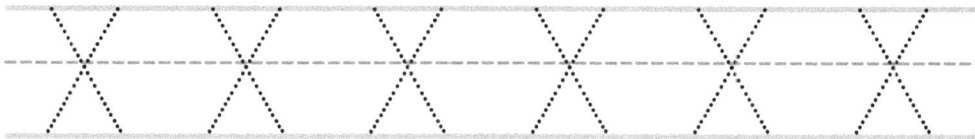

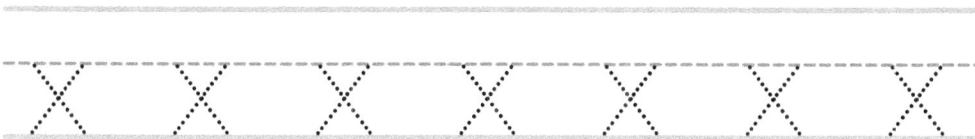

X X X X X X

Trace the letters with a pencil.

X X X X X X X

Trace the letters with a pencil.

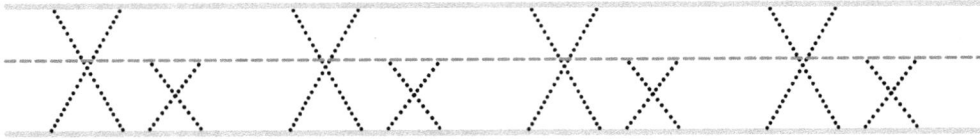

Xx Xx Xx Xx

X

X

X

X

Instructions: Have your child trace the word, say the word out loud, and help to read the definition of each word. You can even hang this on their wall or mirror to say each day as a daily affirmation.

X

I am...

X-factor

Definition: Noteworthy quality or talent.

Excited

Definition: Very enthusiastic and eager about something.

Exquisite

Definition: Very beautiful or delicate.

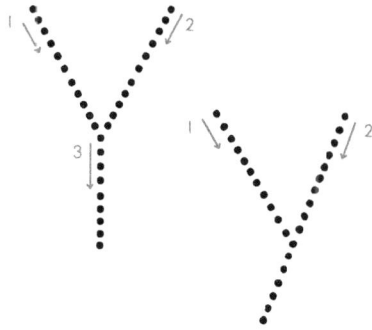

Y y

is for yoga.

Trace the letters with a pencil.

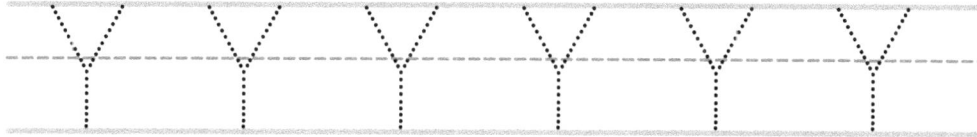

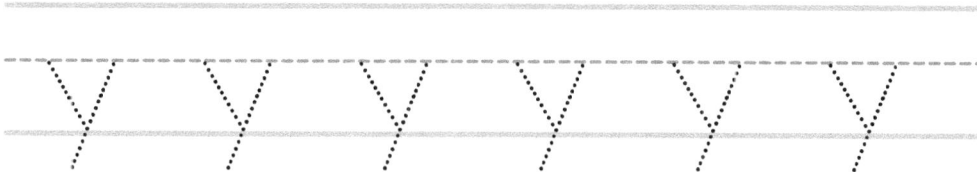

Y Y Y Y Y Y

Trace the letters with a pencil.

y y y y y y

Trace the letters with a pencil.

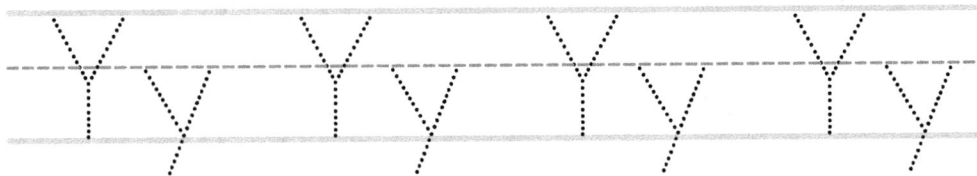

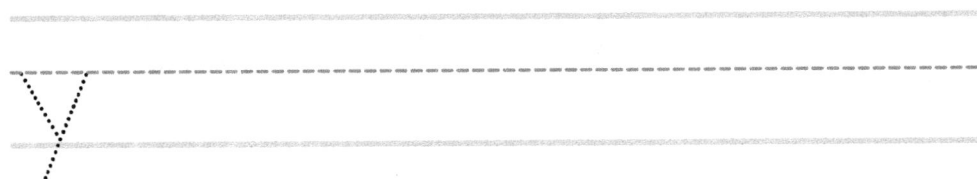

Y y Y y Y y Y y

Y

Y

Y

y

Instructions: Have your child trace the word, say the word out loud, and help to read the definition of each word. You can even hang this on their wall or mirror to say each day as a daily affirmation.

Y

I am...

Youthful

Definition: Having or showing the innocence and hope of someone who is young.

Yielding

Definition: Tending to do or willing to do what other people want.

Yearning

Definition: To want something very much.

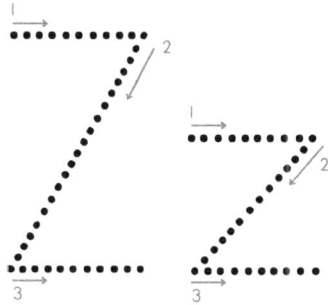

is for zebra.

Trace the letters with a pencil.

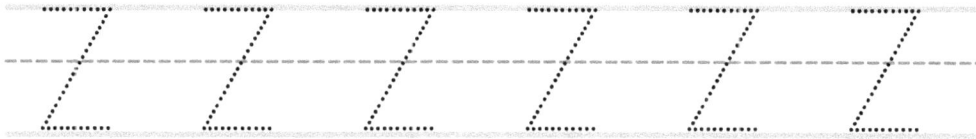

Trace the letters with a pencil.

Trace the letters with a pencil.

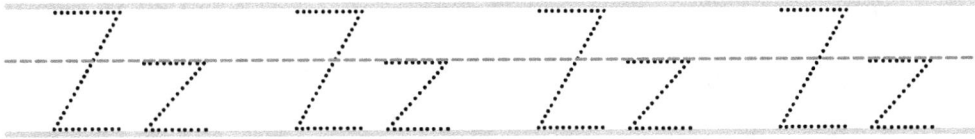

Zz Zz Zz Zz Zz Zz Zz

Z

Z

Z

Z

Instructions: Have your child trace the word, say the word out loud, and help to read the definition of each word. You can even hang this on their wall or mirror to say each day as a daily affirmation.

Z

I am...

Zealous

Definition: Feeling or showing strong and energetic support for a person or cause.

Zestful

Definition: Lively; a feeling of enjoyment.

Zippy

Definition: Very fast; appealingly stylish.

Kyla Thompson

Kyla Thompson